PURPLE PEARLS

PURPLE PEARLS

love, lust and loss

Claudia McKenzie

tgh.

LONDON

Purple Pearls: love, lust, and loss

The book information is catalogued as follows;
Author Name(s): Claudia McKenzie
Title: Purple Pearls: love, lust, and loss

Description; First Edition
1st Edition, 2021

Book Design by Leah Kent

ISBN 978-1-914447-30-3 (paperback)
ISBN 978-1-914447-31-0 (ebook)

Prepared by That Guy's House
www.ThatGuysHouse.com

Thank you to
my mother (Myrtle)

My daughter (Shanyah)

My sister (Keisha)

And the greatest friends
(Colis, Kizzy, Lorraine, Natasha, Melissa M and Emma B)

Thank you for walking next to me
in the rain, through thunderstorms, and the sunshine rays
sometimes with tears and fears
sometimes with a belly full of laughter

thank you for being my journey
and inspiring me to live a full life

When your heart has lived through poverty
you learn that
only the love
and kindness you give yourself
can feed and satisfy your soul

contents

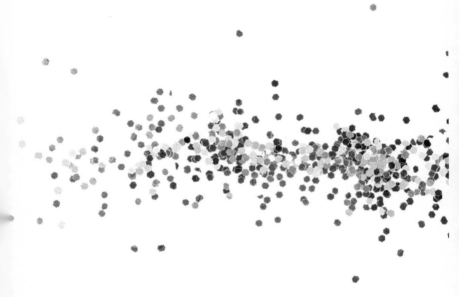

For the love of lust

Purple Pearls

I suppose you could say I found my way back home

The journey was not always lonely
sometimes I danced with the old man who had a song
to fill the holes in my bones
A key to a bed to warm my swollen soul

I found a map that spun me in circles
took me on the wrong track and I ended up on my
back
by the riverside I washed my feet and prayed

The moon came
The sun rose
I was still all alone

The men came to rescue me
Their touches eased my lust for love
One by one I let them in
One by one they left again
Each time they took a piece of me on their lips

The moon came
The sun rose
I was still all alone

I knew there was a home for me
I climbed and climbed my way
to a land I did not recognize
His warm flesh was where I rested my head
In time he rode the waves my hips
he fed from my honey lips
he danced in my arms
he made promises that he had an African drum that
could beat life into a home
I believed
I followed him
Home
He laid purple pearls at my feet
he said he accepted my complexity, my passion
he accepted me
I was all I had to be

the moon came
the sun rose
I was no longer alone

We laughed for years
He became my country
He became my home

On the last day of autumn, his footsteps were all that
he left behind
Every day I prayed for my body to pour my soul back
into my skin
for nine months I lived under the moon
I missed my home

The moon came
Our son rose
I had grown flesh and
I had grown a heartbeat from our home
I had found my way back home

My filthy little mind
convinced my foolish heart
that my body could
feed the poverty in your eyes

my foolish heart
fed you from my bones
until there was
nothing left
of my filthy little mind

I was brutal
in loving him
and
beautifully scared
from chasing him

we laugh
we cry
we fall apart

we laugh
we cry
we realize we
cannot be apart

If I love you any harder
I am sure I will fade away

I love you beneath your feet
I love you under your sheets
Folding
Bending
I turn my inside into you

If I love you any harder
I am sure I will fade away

She loved the sensation of sugary Saturday nights
she loved the darkness of the night
it was where she learnt to hide her light
she drank from the cloudy well of men
she swallowed them to feed her thirst
she couldn't resist the poison
from each hand that fed her body

in the darkest part of the night
she allowed the men with meaningless names to
balance their dirty feet and hard foreign
bodies against her chest
she waited patiently as they dug from her roots
searching for what she could not describe and
what they could not find

Sunday morning would begin with her stuffing her gut
with shame and regret for breakfast
and the soles of men's feet imprinted in her
history

He wanted to kiss her hand
share his plans
he offered her something new
he tried to open the crack in her mind to let the light in
but the girl wanted her heart to remain blue
she liked the sound of her tears crashing through her
chest, the way they rest on the edges of her heart
she liked the dark clouds in her hair

so, she hid when he got near
his careless breathing
his light gave her a fright

she seeks comfort by cutting her skin and
letting the pain in
she had no room in her mind to trust
something new
pain was all she knew

He asked if he could steal a kiss
from her lips
with bloodstained lips
and pieces of the other girl's skin
dangling from his teeth

I wrestled with your demons like they were all mine
I hugged your pain
gave the attention like they were all mine

I learned every dark corner of your thoughts
I made them comfortable in my home
when the world was dark, we stayed home

I made friends with the devils who walked by your side
I agreed when they said darkness was paradise

I tried to cover the cracks in your soul
with my love
with my body
with my all the promises in the world
but nothing was enough to stop your bleeding heart

My love
I did it because I loved you
I did it because I wanted all of you
I tried to bend your spine with my promises and lies
when that didn't work
I tried to twist your heart with tattoos of reasons we
should part
when that didn't work
I tried to cut pieces of your feet with reasons why you
could not leave
when that didn't work
I gave you a blow to the head
hoping you would be dead
then begging you not to leave

I asked you if I am pretty
My heart, my ego and I had spent moments before
smiling and imagined you would correct me
and tell me I am beautiful
instead
with black pearls in your eyes
you ask
"What has pretty got to do with you.? Flowers are
pretty"

-seeking validation

There is an enchanting song
my soul likes to sing
when he dances inside of me

-lust

If I could tell you
I would let you know
my heart crazy for you
sometimes I think I love you

if I could tell you
I would let you know
early in the morning
my mind is full of you

if I could tell you
I would let you know
I have written a love song
just for you
I would ask you to listen
to all the reasons why I think I love you

I closed my eyes and listened
to the melody of his sweet words
apologies mixed with empty promises
he begged
I played hard to get

his touch felt like cocoa butter on my skin
the warmth of him
smooth and comforting
there really was no need for him to pull me in
I was his

I opened my eyes
there he was
the devil in disguise
tall, beautiful, and strong
lips soft and sweeter than the darkest berries
his kisses, the scent of early spring

I smiled
I accepted his lies
I promised myself
this would be the last time

-beautiful liar

I asked him for love
He offered me sex

I asked him for commitment
He offered to pay a month's rent

I asked him for respect
He offered to see her less

I asked him to leave
He offered to stay if only to play

When the hummingbirds are asleep, and the moon
makes its way to me
I dream
I dream
I dream of every inch of you
I wait
I wait
I wait and follow the moon to you

I waited for the hummingbirds to sing
I waited for the sun to rise
I waited for the flowers to bloom
I waited for the moon to glow

I waited for your love to return
I waited
I waited
I wait

I think someone told life that I liked it rough
Or perhaps my grandmother's mother made plans with
the universe to
make me tough
by strengthening my back
with love made from rocks
to carve me into a woman
with the strength of an ox

My man
My man is tall,
dark and lean
he smells so clean

his walk is smooth and silky clean
his smile a pretty perfection

I sip from the cup that holds my tears
as I consider how such a beautiful man could be so mean

The day I decided
I was taking a break from love

you walked into my life
bright and breezy
with your rich looks
and smelling like paradise

when you spoke
a little explosion of laughter
escaped my lips
and
my greedy heart
could not help herself
she grabbed onto to you
now she will do anything for you

I know you are
poison to my body
but I can't help feeding off
your promises

I hate to be that girl
to question what I mean to you
but you have left
your crisscross footsteps on my bed
is it to remind me of what we shared or maybe just to
play with the thoughts that run through my head?

After a while the crisscross
Disappeared
but
midnight came ten times before I saw you again
deep rivers of your mouth run through my veins
the way you leave vanilla on my lips
I curse and curse and say never again
But my heart is a stubborn fool

The angry mother
Slammed the door behind her lover
warned her daughter
never to bend her arm for a man
never to fall in love
and
reminded her that when you fall
you hurt

Let me tell you about my love
He is like a portrait in the sun
he is like standing on the tip of a mountain,
swallowing the richness of the island where
I am from

he is like birds singing in the rain, with their sweet
melodies dancing through your skin

Let me tell you about my love
he is a million things

he makes me sink into the gully of my
bones when I think he is gone

he makes me shelter from life in his arms
he makes me feel like there is no better
place
when he is home

She wanted it all
she wanted to be beautiful and happy
but she decided maybe next summer
next summer when she is slimmer
when her thighs stopped fighting and
slapping each other
then she would decide to be beautiful
and happy

Why don't you miss me as much as I want
you?

Secret kisses under the mango tree
he held her face in his hands and told her
again, the story of how they will be

Her heart stopped for a moment when her
brown eyes met his
she saw their lives engraved in the bluest
part of his eyes

they say love is blind but, in that moment,
they could see the love in their souls

they danced in the rain
drenched their hopes in the rainbow
the birds giggled as they watched the magic
in their touch

Fatherless daughters
will empty their hearts and bellies
to feed the thirst of a man

His name is charmer on most days
it's all so easy for him
he has smooth lips; they will invite you to
stay and play

charmer is wonderful if I may say
his warmth, his masculinity is drenched in
pretend passion

his gaze will invite you to make gentle
pornography with him
his words are so soft and sweet
you may feel like you would die without him
he has melted many hearts away

but charmer is a stranger, some may say
because charmer will never give his heart
away

You chose to leave
for another love
I chose silence and distance
I chose to forgive
I chose to heal and learn from the hurt
I choose love

One day her heart just got up
and
walked out of her chest

-broken heart

We are the story
that started with a promising beginning
but then
we endured tragedy, suffering and
destruction
we stayed strong
only to find happiness and peace
apart

You left me behind
like an old school jumper
I chased you wildly
like a dandelion chasing a crazy wish

If you cut your flesh
I will bleed

-obsession

The men that came
always seem to believe
the only way to love me
is to water me with their milk and plant me with their
seeds

You touched my face with grace
and made me forget you screamed poisoned words in
my face

you kissed my lips and made me forget you were the
monster who stole my dreams and told me they could
never be

you laid me down and entered the place that made me
forget when I needed you the most
you knocked me further into the ground

you held me close and whispered
you loved me the most
and made me forget how much I regret
the day we met

when you left the woman inside
the one I used to be, cried

I choked back her voice
She screams and begs me
not to forget

-toxic love

Last night while I was talking to the black moon
A star giggled
and told me my rainbow wishes to dance with you
made her laugh

Do not mistake the quiet fire in your thoughts as
harmless smoke
one day you may find your whole body on fire

-unresolved trauma

The banana tree bent its leaves
around her
to protect and hold her
to set her free
helplessly
all it could do was watch as he
pulled
twisted
her little knees
apart
and drenched himself
in her innocence
searching for something
she did not have to give

You seasoned your tongue
with sweet words
I gladly swallowed each one
letter by letter
as they leaked from your lips
In hope that they would feed
my hunger for love
but they just left my heart burning

My friends spent hours
cursing and hating you
and I joined in too

but when my friends
and the wine were gone
I sat alone
and thought about
how much I ache for you
how much I miss and love you

I want to call you a liar
but then I remembered
you did show me who you are
and warned me I was playing with fire
I decide I my life could handle the flames

I want to say you betrayed me
but then I remembered
It was me who chose to stay
every time you bruised my heart
and put the blame on me
I chose to stay

I want to say I don't want you
but every minute of my day
is filled with thoughts of you
and all the ways to make you love
me the right way

I spread my love
all over you
like peanut butter
on fresh bread
I hoped you would
enjoy the taste and ask
for more
but you simply licked
your lips and ran
out the door

You should allow your pain to walk through
your flesh and speak to your bones
It often has an important message for your
heart

I used my body to cover you
in the winter

I tried to crack the sky open
to find the sun to warm your heart

when the summer came
you left me for money and fame

-used

My raging roots
wanted to dig up the earth
from under your feet
just to watch you fall apart
for breaking my heart

I love the quietness
of your hands
I love the loudness
of your heart

I love the softness
of your words
I love the fierceness
of your commitment

I will win

I will fight
I will fight

I will win the fight
I will win back what you took from my heart

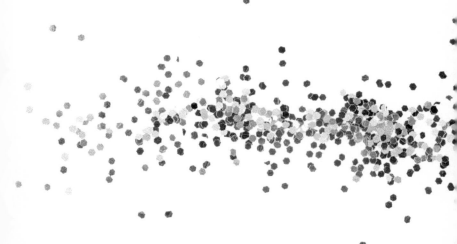

Anxiety

"Forgive me" he begged

I watched my uncle on his death bed
death refusing to pleasure his mind
pain refusing to let his body rest

I watched as he struggled to breathe
the same way I had struggled many times as
he stole parts of me
I watched as he vomited his ugly sins onto his
mother's heart

"Forgive me" he begged

I watched as his unwashed mouth moved in
slow motion
Dripping salty poison over his mother's feet

"Forgive me" he begged

I watched as he counted his regrets
trying to find words to pay his debts
but his dirty words tangled in his neck

"Forgive me" he begged

I watched as he loaded his mother's head with
his truth
like a loaded gun
I watched as he shot her in the head with all
he had done

I watched as she begged him to stop
just the way I had done
"Forgive me" he begged

I watched as she got up and ran
I watched as his misery swallowed him alive
I watched as he reaped what he sowed

The day the hurricane came
I was minding my own business
tidying the house
washing the dishes
folding the clothes
a little bit of ironing
and a few other things

I sipped my tea
and thought about cooking

then the memory came
it rose
and took over my body
it dug its way through the earth
where I am sure I left it
bursting its way into my mind
where it settled
and made itself home

there were no introductions
there were no small talks

I crawled on the floor
took cover
I wait and wait
for her to leave
-depression

You try so often to be more than you need to be
You try so often to be everything they want you to be

There is no method to this madness
Let go and be whatever you want to be
It is the only way to be free

Her body thick like mud
Her brain, paper thin and drained

Her fragile fingers played with the plumpness of her
flesh and her mind wished she could wrap it all in a
bag and fling it high

But that was a silly wish
Instead, she ate and ate until she was full of regret
Some days she ate all day to soothe and numb the
shame
To dampen the flames that burn and hurt her chest

She wished she could be that girl
The girl with the beautiful curls that dance along with
her when she moves
The girl who swings her limbs as she climbs the stairs
of life with ease

She was tired of being the girl who could not bend
her knees
The girl she could not please

You ripped at my clothes
But it was my heart that you tore

You parted my flesh
But it was my soul that you pierced

You went inside me
But you were not invited

You wiped the blood from my skin
But it was my heart that was bleeding

You ran away
But you left you stench on me

I smell you everyday

-uninvited

A person with open
unattended wounds
will cry like a wounded wolf
but you will never see a tear drop

How can I be a survivor?
when my hands are not blooded
from fighting back

how can I be a survivor?
my body is not bruised
from the place you entered

how can I be a survivor?
you were not a perfect stranger

-the rape

The night I was born it rained
It rained all day
On the sunniest island in the world
It rained
It rained all day
It was black
It was black all day
It rained
It rained all day
That's what they all day

My journey from my mother's womb took all day
I had her on her back
I had her on her back all day
I split her lips
I cracked her hips
I stopped her heart
she died a few times that day
I had her on her back
I had her on her back all day
That's what they all say

When I was born
I was covered in blood and rage
and I have stayed that way

that's what they all say
it was peaceful agony and chaos for my mother that
day
it was like a bloody murder
that's what they all day
The night I was born it rained
It rained all day
That's what they all say

Then the tears came. It started out as a scream which
then turned into wailing, a big loud ugly noise came
from my mouth, it took over my entire body, I had no
control over it. All the pain I had held inside started to
seep out of me. I cried so hard if you could cry
yourself to death, in that moment I stood next to
death. I cried from deep in my belly, my whole body
shook uncontrollably. I cried for the broken little girl
inside of me. Because it was then I realised how wrong
it all was, what had happened to me. I felt so dirty. I
cried eleven years of pain and fear that I had held
inside. I wanted to crawl out of my skin, out of my
body, my brain. I cried for hours. I cried to free and
cleanse myself from them. I silently cried myself to
sleep that night. The next day I woke up a different
person.

-letting go of hurt

When she cries and asks him why
He smooths her soul
by singing her a lullaby full of lies

You have violently
broken your own heart
again and again

you watched as the sun
quickly clears the tears and clouds from her eyes
to shine bright for all those waiting for her

and
You have fooled yourself
in believing you should be able to do the same

Although you are also a star
You are not the sun
It's ok for you to take your time to put yourself
back together again

I wish I could send my heart
back to heaven
this one is broken
and cannot be mend

Try not to envy her beauty and grace
Inside her there is a quiet riot
a great fire, blazing with hurt
an ocean of confusion
every day she is fighting

I asked death to be my friend
he turned and ran when he saw the
the angel stood next to me

-My child

She wanted to cut the flesh of her skin
to see if the pain would leak out

it took her a while to realize
the hurt was planted much deeper

She showed him
the surface of her pearls
but he said he wanted to get to know her
he asked her to open her pages
afraid
she opened her skin and let him in
she could not trust him
with what she was hiding
beneath her flesh

She drank from the bottle
like she was drinking from a river
the white liquid burns
and silences her fears
numbs and scares
the feelings away
leaving her
comforted

-self medicating

She unzipped her heart in front of him
the truth fell out
he grabbed her
held her
his touch
stopped her from falling apart

The hummingbird became my nurse
from the day you took your words and
squeezed the light out of me

your words live in my throat
your touch lives in the breast of my breath
I breathe only pain and regret

yet my eyes burn with thoughts of you
still my ears hurt from memories of you
forever my heart can only see you

Climbing the hill to discover herself
She found fear along the way
without asking
fear stood beside her
step by step
fear followed
but she kept climbing anyway

It's ok to lose your mind
for a moment
but you must not lose faith
because without faith
you are powerless

The moon knows
when I am depressed
to the rest of the world
I submerge all my stress and regrets
into rainbows and smiles

When I am alone
and about to walk into the shadows
of sleep
she comes to me
at first, she is soft
and her whisper is sweet
I ignored her
I was desperate to feel
the warmth of slumber

her voice becomes a hammer
she likes when I crumble

I try not to shake
I try not to break
she cuts deep into me
with her sordid words
depression she calls herself
some days
but anxiety at times
she makes me play her games
where she makes fun of how great I am
then she reminds me I am out of my mind
still, I can't send her away
she is my obsession
she is my friend
and the one I despise

I used to allow you to hop and off me
the same way I used to hop on and off
London busses

until one day
I slipped
and fell flat on my face

and just like the bus
you did not stop to check on me
you just kept on moving

-bruised ego

I wish I could go back just one minute
just one minute before the grief
just one minute before the truth came out
just one minute before the nothingness settled in

I want to feel the sun kissing my skin
I want to feel pain
I want to feel the blood running through my veins

I wish I could go back just one minute before

-numb

I remember the day my depression escaped from the
cage I locked her in
somehow, she found a way to break free
she walked all over my face
she made my skin grey and plain for all to see
she covered my bed with crazy thoughts
she sank her teeth into my heart
she bit at my lips
she wanted me to cry
I cried and I cried

There is something dark
that happens to a heart
that has had to beg for love

Strong black souls
floating in the air
strong black bodies
suffering in silence

I watch them
as I lay on the doorsteps of rock bottom
floating over me
like stars in the sky
I watch them

in the deepest part of the night
strong black souls
strong black bodies
I see them
I see them floating next to mine

The clarity you so desperately want
will find you
when the time is right
for now
just breathe

Do you remember happiness
the days when there was no fuss
when your head and you heart were not at war

Do you remember happiness
when your thoughts didn't hurt your skin
the days when everything was simple, pretty, and bright
you simply could not wait for the day to start
when you could hear birds chatting and their
conversations warmed your heart

Do you remember happiness?

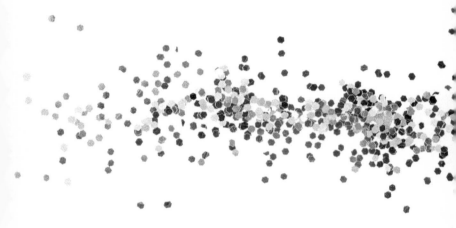

Acceptance

She was born high in the mountains
Into the mouth of poverty

She grew on a lion's back
Sheltered from the rain in the bats cave
She danced with the wolves and became brave

She fed her hunger by living life
with courage and a little bit of fun and play

She lived a rich life

I don't want the designer bag kind of love
The plastic bag kind will do
I want to see all you carry and hold inside of you

-transparency

Like me
the moon knows
what it is like
to have a dark side
and still be beautiful

When you left
I fell to the ground and broke my crown

I felt the pain of a thousand souls
I cried

I begged
I lied
I tried
I cried
I cried a thousand goodbyes
I screamed
I begged
I prayed and prayed to God to make a way for you to
stay

It took me a thousand days
A thousand way
A thousand tries
A thousand whispers of love from those who cared
They gave me a thousand reasons to stay alive

When I could breathe
With ease
That was when you came back with your lies

Looking pleased
You cried
You begged
You lied
You tried
You cried a thousand times

She found
the truth
in his lies

-boys

Happiness
Cannot live without
Love

She wanted to be a sunflower
Until she remembered
she grew best in the shadows

He left
a note
on my gold nightstand
it said "I am sorry, it's not you, it's me"

I am guessing he has chosen himself
not me

Did you know the devil has beautiful hands?
Hands that will create magic in your heart
magic that turns love into quiet violence
so subtle you will not see it coming until you are
fighting flames to protect your bones

Not every woman needs
to experience pain
as women
when we share what we have learnt
from our hurt
We should pass these pearls of wisdom to women and
girls
to save them from what we know will break them

There will never be a day
without darkness
And
There will never be a day
without light
Both are temporary
Do not be afraid of the dark

If you can find peace in your skin
and in your heart at the break of day
and
still hold onto it in the heat of the day
you have found happiness

The truth
no longer burns
my adult skin

Every day when you open your eyes
and while you wait for your skin to heal
step into the day with gratitude on your mind
make your thoughts easy on the tongue
use your toughness to soften hearts
you might get a surprise
when you realize you
being alive is worthwhile

Maybe some day
You will find that love isn't grey

Maybe someday
Thorns will no longer grow from your heart

Maybe someday
you will accept
that the stars and the moon
are not the only ones who are there
for you

The only enemy
you need to fight
is the one within you
that keeps you second guessing
your power and your worth

Self-love is still choosing
to love fully
even when
your heart is in broken pieces

He crawled to the doctor's room
on his belly
when his legs refused to carry
the weight of his brokenness

-therapy

Time did not heal the pain
the river I cried
did not cleanse you from my skin
thoughts of you
keep bleeding into my brain
into my veins   .
over and over again
when
when will you end?

Although it is not possible
to edit the past pages of your life
you can go back
reread and learn from the lines you missed

I am learning to accept the truth
that our love will never end
but we will never be together

-twin flame

She wanted to be friends with the rainbow
But the rainbow turned her back
And said "I am sorry, but you are black. You are too
overpowering to rock with the rest of my flock"
Rejected, she decided to dance with the storm
And together, they created thunder and lightening

-self-acceptance

Grief is a sign
that you have loved
with every inch of your being

Life can be a crazy heap of mess
you can choose to clean up the mess
by yourself
or allow your loyal
and equally messy friends
to help you

The secrets I held inside
tortured my mind
wrinkled my skin
and played ball with my soul
freedom came
when I unlocked the cage
I held them in

Laying on the grass of my ground floor flat
listening to the voices in my head
trying my hardest not to crack
I know where I need to go
I know what I need to do
to find my way back and elevate my soul
I am doing the work to make my soul better
I learning to forgive my father
so that I can stop searching for him in the dark

Hate is a word we use
when heart broken

hate is an exaggeration of pain
and the many of times we have been hurt

hate is sometimes used
to medicate our bruised ego

During your healing
there will be those days
where you wake up
feeling ugly and unworthy
your spirit low
and your spirit funky

There will be those days
where you feel like
you are falling apart before the day
even starts

There will be those days
where your mind
insists on taking a walk down memory lane
reminding you
of how you have been working so hard
to erase the stains
and you find yourself wondering
was it all in vain?

on those days
draw strength from remembering
healing has layers
layers that will shed like skin
and in time your wounds will heal

My mother was a hunter
a girl in a crowded world
where she stood alone
although not fully grown
at fifteen she became my Queen
my mother
my sole provider
she would snap anyone who tried to fight her

My mother was a fighter
a warrior
she fought her way
through mud and sand
through the thickness of hate
she ran and ran

her bravery became her shield
as she demolished the men who tried
to grab her wrong

on the wings of hope
she flew to a land
where they say the streets are paved with gold
but she found something better than gold
she found freedom
she found a home

Stop postponing your life
find a way to heal
fight
survive
fight
strive

I asked her
how do you make butterflies
dance in your belly and
fly from your thighs like sunrise?

how do you grow roses
from your lips
and feed beautiful men
from your hips

we were cut from the same flesh
we grew in the same nest
where is the magic in my flaws

-sisters

I have learnt if you don't forgive
You will forever be stuck
in the memory of the hurt

it's exhausting trying to muster
the strength
to deal with the pain of yesterday

to deal with the debris in the heart
we must forgive

You are everything
that frightens me

I ransacked your heart
to find something wrong with you

I push you to the edge
to see if you would fall for me

-falling in love

I stretched my arms
to meet the distance
of your heart

I broke a limb
to stop you from sinking
I am glad I stretched
it is the most beautiful
and endless
love I have ever felt

She doesn't pour from her cup
to feed worries from yesterday

she takes pride in her strides
she floats on air into the morning sun
she hunts her dreams until the day is done

-self confidence

There was so much madness and chaos
in finding a soft love like this
when all along it was attached to my skin

I have worked hard
to become soft
in my thoughts when I think of you

-the ex

I want to taste the sweetness of life
I want to feel the bitterness of life
for it is the only way to know when
I am experiencing true love

Tell your secrets to the moon
make it doom and gloom
make it a fairy tale
make it a win
make it fail
whatever you do
tell your secrets
even if it is to someone new

You changed your hair
you changed the clothes you wear
you changed the fact that you said you wanted to be
alone
you even changed the place you call home

but when you are alone
you cannot erase me from your bones

-trauma

Life is not short
when you live
in the dark
life is everlasting
and hard

You cannot jump over your trauma or skip that page in your life story, you must work your way through it to make sense of the next chapter

.

In the quietest part of the night
where it is
just calm darkness
where you can really feel your heart
beating with aches
that is where you will find the magic to heal

I get my confidence
from the colour of my skin
my melanin has dragged me through heat
and rage of unknown hearts
made me work and stay behind till late
just to prove I did not belong in a cage

but I wear my crown on my head
I am proud
I stand up straight
I am reminded to be brave

The colour of my skin
reminds me I came from
a long line of women who are strong
women of faith
women who forgive
even when the pain has been left on their skin

I went to find love
I took a chance
I followed his footsteps down by the sea
where the moon glows

the palm trees
played hide and seek with the breeze
I drank the words from your lips
I took your ring
and I said yes to everything

You have just climbed
Through the valley of death
You have just made it through
the battle of your life
fought a tough war with yourself

and although the chains
are still visible around your neck
you have made it out alive

it is only sensible to rest
take your doctor's advice
allow her to tend to your wounds
follow her orders to heal
your injured parts
do all that is necessary to avoid infections

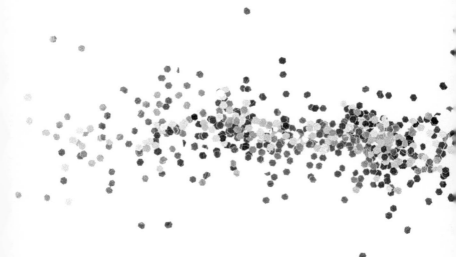

Growth

Brown girl
Brown girl, teach me how to look like you do
Teach me the magic spell you use to make your skin
glow and sparkle like gold dust

Even as the whips they have placed on your back shine
with scars

Brown girl
Brown girl, teach me how to walk like you
Teach me how walk with grace and confidence

Even as you make your way through the valley of the
shadow of death

Brown girl
Brown girl, teach me how to love with faith like you
Teach me how to comfort and embrace

Even as you brush the dust and ashes from the flesh of
your heart as you bleed and fall apart from the pain of
those who betrayed you and tried to burn you

Women who wear purple purples
can walk in their naked truth
unapologetically

they choose to be brave when the world tries to oil their
skin with endless shame
they know they cannot watch flowers
grow from their grave

they choose to fight with their light
the pain they carry in their arms like soldiers fade with
antidotes of love and forgiveness
they walk through life on their ancestors prays
fearlessly
they walk through life with pride
they choose to stay alive

their legs may have been spread a little too wide
by unwanted eyes
but they keep their heads held high
they have learnt to leave old hates at the
foot of the moon

from her lips love is spread
from her hips children are held
she fertilizes the world with her joy

Forgive them
So that you do not take them to bed with you

Forgive them
So that thoughts of them do not run streams through
your sheets

Forgive them
So that images of them do not follow you to sleep and
haunt your dreams

Forgive them
So that you can sleep and be free

My healing started
when I closed my legs
and opened my heart
to the possibility
that I was worth more
than what my body could give him

While I waited for my bones to heal
You held my hand
You became my father, a great provider and protection
You became my mother, a home full of warmth and
kindness
You became my grandmother, a song of sweet lullabies
You became my grandfather, a page of wisdom
You became my brother, my big defender

You became my sister, a journal of secrets to share
You became my lover and my friend, a hug filled
with compassion

And most of all, you became silent when I needed to
hear my own voice

-healing

No
I do not want to play
I do not want to chase
you
I do not want to taste
you
Do not whisper memories into my eyes
Please keep your tangled words and dripping lips
closed
You have dipped your salt into too many pots of honey
I have my own honey
I do not want to taste theirs on my lips

-the liar

I like how love
tickles my lips with laughter

I collect rejections in my purse
like they are coins for the parking meter
sometimes they make a mess, they scratch and hurt
still, I collect them like evidence
I especially like to collect the ones that stains and sting
my chest
I keep them close as a great reminder for the day when
I no longer need to prove my worth

You make me smile
But
Happiness is for me to find

The sun kissed the sky good morning
the breeze woke the trees
by gently swaying their leaves

The birds washed their feet
In the morning dew while singing
Their sweet melody
Thankful for the morning glory

-life

You rained your sadness all over me
Soaked through to my skin

You left me drowning in the liquid drops
of your pain and shame
until one day I realized I was not to blame

-emotional vampires

His eyes point out how desirable
I am to him
the words that leaked
from his thick lips
make it clear
he would like to ride
the rhythm of my hips

and

perhaps
I would have entertained his foolishness
If he was not dripping in sin

-the married man

Sing from your belly
Laugh from your heart
Free yourself from within
Dig deep and begin to live hard
You deserve it all

He often says I no longer know how to have a laugh
Unbeknown to him
When I am alone
I laugh
I laugh
I laugh my belly full
I laugh a laugh that turns into a gut-wrenching cry

Nevertheless
I laugh
I laugh
I laugh my belly full
at how funny it is that he does not realise
he is in this relationship alone

every thought
every decision
is made by him
is made for him

every touch
is unjust

I laugh
I laugh
I laugh my belly full
It is funny how he does not realize
my absence
I left him long a go
It is only my body next to him

I will laugh
I will laugh
I will laugh my belly full
Until the day my feet find the courage to walk in a
straight line
Part of life's journey is realizing that whatever it is that
is tying you up in knots
has already been done and you cannot undo it.
Be honest with yourself
Loosen the rope
accept there is hope

Plant yourself like a mango tree
in the middle of an orange grove
and stand firm in your uniqueness

There is no such thing as a wise fool
So do not dismiss the pearls of wisdom life has dropped
at your feet
When you know better, you do better
You ask for better and you demand better for yourself

The scars beneath my skin
the scars tattooed on my heart
the scars etched in my head
have given me the power to reach high
and the grace to land soft

Nothing can hit you as hard as life
the trick is to remember that the pain is temporary
something I wish I had remembered in the middle of
the storms that I have weathered.
These experiences have taught me to take comfort in
knowing that nothing, absolutely nothing lasts forever

Black girl
I see you walking in harmony
Stepping in the rhythm of your spirit
Sprinkling your magic everywhere you go

I am the exploding feeling in your chest
after a kiss

I am the soft smile in your voice
when you speak

I am the carelessness
in your footsteps

I am the tingle in your fingertips
I am the butterfly feeling
in the pit of your belly

I am your future
I am love

Put down that heavy load which you have wrapped up
in shame, blame and guilt
you have been carrying around with you for so long
to banish the darkness and shadows
put down that heavy load
if your life constantly feels like inky black nights, but
you know that it is possible for them to change to sunny
bright days.
Where you can live and thrive
put down that heavy load

Why do you keep holding and petting your dreams?
they are not meant to keep your hands warm
set them free, they have work to do
give them the power to bring magic and change
to the world

Self-love is realising
that you are perfectly enough
to spend time by yourself
and enjoy the sound of your own laughter

You will find your way
through the shadows
open up
let the light drench your sore eyes
open up and give your skin a chance to breath
learn the lines of your scars
and
allow your ancestral wisdom
to guide you
from the darkness
into the sun

Self-love is being kind
to the little girl inside of you
and listening to her needs

Fall in love
but do not give your heart or your soul away

watch as the sun paints itself gold
but do not try to shine in the same way
let love grow
and glow from your soul

Self-love is
finding inner peace
after a lifelong
war with your own flesh

I have learnt the hard way
if you try to fix
a broken person
you will end up with a broken heart

Don't ignore the flowers
growing from your roots
just because
they are surrounded by weeds

My grandmother told me
to never forget to laugh
she said
when your face is full
of life
you should
suffocate your body with joy
laugh and laugh some more

she said when life was good
to her face
when the years took too long
to disappear
and she craved to be more in years
she wished
she had taken the time
to play and seek more in life, to watch
the sun rise and say hello to the moon

she wished she had laughed
and laugh some more

What hurts you now
will guide you to make
better choices tomorrow

Fall in love
with someone who will
use respectful words
to argue with you
even when you fill them
with a belly full of fire

It's not my birthday
it's not our anniversary
it's not Christmas
it's not a special occasion

but you still made me breakfast in bed
with six dozen yellow roses

its not the small things
it's not the big things
it's not the typically romantic things

it is the sweet air of your beauty
it is the daily nourishment
you give to my heart

When a marriage is over
or the one you love
more than your own skin
is over you
the years and the love have slipped
through your fingers
it will feel like life is over

allow yourself to grieve
accept that you must divorce yourself
from the old version of you
become single
get to know you again
and create a new you

Think like a queen
and
let fear hold your hand and guide you
let hope sit on your chest or just beside you
talk less and let your feet say more
breathe and let love flow

If you have lived
you have craved love
and
living life
as an imperfect person
searching for love
in time you will learn
that your beauty cannot feed his skin
your salty tears can wash away your fears
you are likely to be heart broken by life
but you must continue to live
you have enough love of your own to survive

I want to thank God for the day we met
thank him for the time we have spent
today, yesterday and the rest

I want to thank you
for helping me feel
the sunshine on my face
thank you for helping me
with the stress and pain of life
you are always next to me
ready to fight

thank you for loving me unconditionally
thank you for sharing your
thoughts and dreams with me

I know some days we argue and fight
but I know if we are together
the sky will never fall
thank you for sharing your heart

When life has flung you
to the furthest distance
and you have hit rock bottom
it's ok to lay perfectly still for a while
cuddle the pain and give it some attention
but you must let it go
set it free

I love London
not just any part of London
I love South London

I will never forget the day I was walking through the
crowd
(In between the busses and the men who tried to sell
me their plans for us to have a good time)
from Elephant and Castle to Old Kent Road
when I came across an old man
with sand in his hand
he was sitting on the grass in Burgess Park

his white shirt was neatly pressed
and clung to his bony chest
his brown eyes were coffee warm
he was looking to the sky
I decided to approach him and say hi

I asked him why he had sand in his hands
he smiled
and asked me to open my hands
he stretched out his long arm like a giraffe stretching its
neck to feed me

he poured the sand into the palm of my hands
and said "sometimes you may not have any plans, but
God always has plans for you. This is not sand, it is
gold. I have been waiting for the one who would be
kind enough to take the time to smile and talk with me
for a while. I am blind but I can see you have a
priceless soul and I have a bag full of solid gold. I want
you to take it and make plans. Make a difference. Help
a child to rise, help a man to become a King, help a
woman to cleanse the hurt and hate from her heart. Or
just use it to make yourself a ring. Whatever you do, do
not waste your blessing. You have a heart full of gold."

Before you burn your self
change your mind
you do not need to bloody your heart
to make him understand your worth?

We all have a story about love
when you are not prepared for the cost
of finding love
you will burn
you will die a thousand times
the pain will echo in your footsteps
you will grieve
you will not forget
you will have many regrets
but
when you discover the amazement of yourself
you will learn
you will heal
you will accept you are not done yet
you will grow
you will love like you have never loved before

About the Author

Claudia was born in Jamaica, where her life had been turbulent and troubled.

She had experienced sexual and physical abuse as a child, but this shaped her to become a survivor.

At the tender age of 13, Claudia moved to Wiltshire, United Kingdom with her mother. Here, she dealt with the challenges of being a shy and secretly traumatised girl. Claudia spent most of her adult life living in South London. She experienced lust, love and loss.

This is Claudia's first collection of poetry which reflects her life and her experiences.

Instagram: @iamclaudiamckenzie
Facebook: Claudia McKenzie
Tiktok: @claudiamckenziepoetry

Lightning Source UK Ltd.
Milton Keynes UK
UKHW010623250122
397668UK00001B/198